# GUID[illegible]

# RECONSTRUCTIONS

# OF

# VILLA ADRIANA

# AND VILLA D'ESTE

BY

CHIARA MORSELLI

Drawings and Reconstructions: Vision s.r.l. - STM - Roma
Photographs: Vision s.r.l.
Layout: U. Ulivieri
English Translation by Vision s.r.l.

# HADRIAN'S VILLA

## THE EMPEROR HADRIAN

Hadrian, who was of spanish origin like his predecessor and tutor Trajan who had adopted him right before his death, was proclaimed Emperor in 117 A.D. at the age of forty.

"He was tall of stature and elegant in appearance; his hair was curled on a comb, and he wore a full beard to cover up the natural blemishes on his face; and he was very strongly built. He rode and walked a great deal and always kept himself in training by the use of arms and the javelin. He was, in the same person, austere and genial, dignified and playful, dilatory and quick to act, niggardly and generous, deceitful and straightforward, cruel and merciful".

*Portrait of the emperor Hadrian*

Thus a later biographer of the *Historia Augusta* (IV century A.D.) describes the physical appearance and character of Hadrian, who was a man with a multiform personality, a clever, cultured and illuminated organizer of the Empire of which for twenty years he governed the destiny, as well as being authoritarian and ambitious.

He was a careful administrator of the state apparatus, renewing appointments and functions, creating a decentralised juridical system and developing the role of controlling magistrates for public finances.

Concerning the Provinces that he visited several times, Hadrian promoted a policy of abandoning those territories that were to be considered as not possible to defend (like Armenia, Assiria and Mesopotamia) and defined a new defensive system of the frontiers. The *Vallum* or wall that he built in Britannia and which was named after him, is without doubt the most complete and noteworthy defensive system of the whole Roman age.

He was therefore a man of peace and he promoted urban projects which were aimed at consolidating and developing the spreading of Romanity. He founded new cities in Egypt, in Asia Minor, in Thrace; he built new roads and bridges in Gaul. He was a philhellenic Emperor who did his best to raise the economic level of Greece and he financed important public works in Athens.

In Rome also, the age of Hadrian was a period of very intensive building, with the construction of buildings with great architectural significance (like the

*Model of Hadrian's Villa*

Pantheon, the Temple of Venus and Rome, the Mausoleum) where classical traditions and new trends coexist and which characterize all of Hadrian's architecture; Hadrian's villa is the most complete expression of this style.

Hadrian died in 138 A.D. at the age of sixty two, appointing Antoninus Pius as his successor.

## THE HISTORY OF THE VILLA

The villa is situated on a small plain extending on the slopes of the Tiburtine Hills, south-east of Tivoli, a town not far from Rome, which adds to a pleasant climate the quality of a smiling landscape of quiet beauty enlivened by hills and valleys.

The site chosen for the Imperial residence had first been occupied by a villa of the Republican age (end of the II - beginning of the Ist centuries B.C.), which might have been an inheritance of the wife of the Emperor, Vibia Sabina; from this older nucleus, that was incorporated in Hadrian's project, the subsequent complex was developed.

The historical and artistical importance of Hadrian's creation contrasts with the practically total silence of the contemporary literary sources. A paragraph of Hadrian's biography in the *Historia Augusta* mentions that the Emperor wished to call the various parts of the Villa with the names of the famous places and monuments that he had visited, like the Pecile, the Academy, the Pritaneo and the Lyceum of Athens, the Valley of Tempe in Thessaly, the Canopus

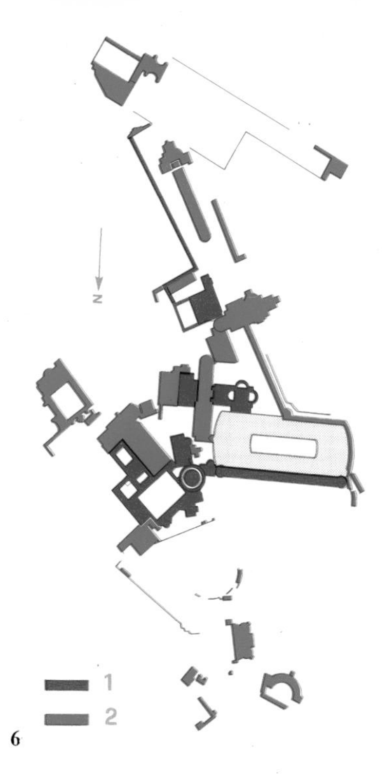


*Building Phases of the Villa*

in Egypt. Names, still used today, that scholars of past centuries gave to various buildings of the complex without any real grounds, with the only exception of the Canopus. The paragraph in reality, reflects Hadrian's great interest and passion for travel, which led him to visit the vast territories of he Empire, of which he was not only a tireless admirer, attracted as he was by the beauty of nature and by the traditions of humanity, but also a careful organizer.

Another legend which is groundless, but seconded by a phrase of the 7th century A.D. historian, Aurelio Vittore, says that the villa was built during the last years of the Emperor's life. On the contrary, the complex was built during the first years of his reign. A detailed study of the buildings has given precise dates inasmuch their chronology is concerned, allowing to recognize two phases of construction, marked by the big journeys of the Emperor to his provinces, the first between the years 118 and 123 A.D., the other from 125 to 133 A.D. On the other hand the fast immediate starting of the works leads to believe that the plan had already been clearly defined for some time and that Hadrian himself could have assisted in its study. Indeed the sources say that the Emperor took delight in practising in architecture and science, demanding that he play a major role in the architectural decisions and in solving technical problems. In this connection their is the famous quotation from the historian Dione Cassio where he tells of the violent argument with the famous Apollodorus of Damascus, who had been

Trajan's Architect, and whose extreme criticisms of Hadrian's projects cost him his life.

At the time of the Emperor's first departure throughout the Empire (121 A.D.) the works concerning the Imperial Palace's englobing of the republican villa, the Maritime Theatre, the neighbouring Hall of the Philosophers and the Heliocaminus Baths had been terminated; during Hadrian's absence the Pecile, the Nymphaeum stadium and the adjoining complexes, the Lesser and Large Baths were completed. Many work sites were opened before his second departure (128 A.D.); the Libraries, the Academia, the Guest Rooms and the Hundred Chambers which were followed by the large *triclinium* complexes of the Piazza d'Oro and of the Canopus. Upon the final return of Hadrian in 134 A.D. the villa had been completed.

Some small restorations and limited modifications are proof of its continued use after Hadrian's death. But his successors chose to reside in Rome and the enormous complex on the Via Tiburtina was used only for vacations. Abandoned and stripped of its works of art maybe even as of the IIIrd century A.D., the Villa fell into oblivion. In 1450 after many centuries of silence, during which the site had been used as a quarry for marble and bricks, the imposing and suggestive ruins were identified with the villa of Hadrian.

# HADRIAN'S VILLA GENERAL PLAN

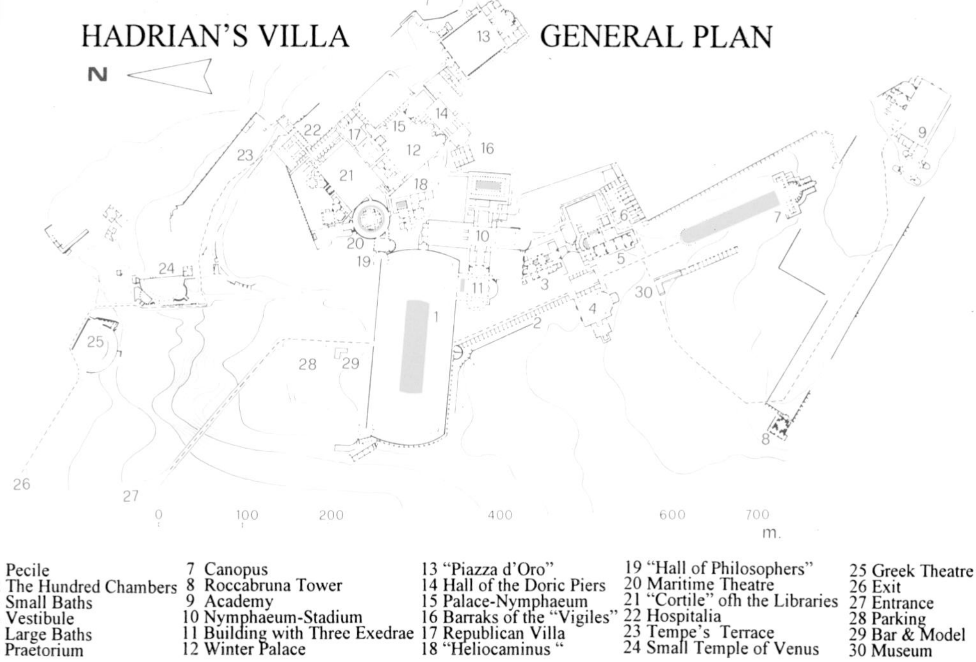


Pecile
The Hundred Chambers
Small Baths
Vestibule
Large Baths
Praetorium

7 Canopus
8 Roccabruna Tower
9 Academy
10 Nymphaeum-Stadium
11 Building with Three Exedrae
12 Winter Palace

13 "Piazza d'Oro"
14 Hall of the Doric Piers
15 Palace-Nymphaeum
16 Barraks of the "Vigiles"
17 Republican Villa
18 "Heliocaminus "

19 "Hall of Philosophers"
20 Maritime Theatre
21 "Cortile" ofh the Libraries
22 Hospitalia
23 Tempe's Terrace
24 Small Temple of Venus

25 Greek Theatre
26 Exit
27 Entrance
28 Parking
29 Bar & Model
30 Museum

## THE GENERAL PLAN AND ARCHITECTURAL CHARACTERISTICS

The complex which covers an area of about 120 hectares, is configured as an immense garden-park, inlaid with monumental and apparently isolated groups of buildings of different orientation. The enormous extension, the quantity of buildings, the originality and complexity of the architectural forms make Hadrian's Villa a unique monument in the history of ancient architecture.

The perfect fusion of architectural structures and large garden-park spaces, only apparently casual, but in fact on the contrary, the fruit of a careful study of the sites, of studied search for landscaping effects, of deep transformation of the natural lie of the ground bent to the needs of precise spatial and structural requirements.

The result is a harmonious and organic complex of carefully planned buildings. Everything is grandiose and painstakingly calculated: It is the permanent residence of the Emperor, his palace for receptions; to be used for official ceremonies, for festivities, banquets, and spectacles for the more important guests, but at the same time a place for retreat, quietness and tranquillity.

Nothing is casual, in the most noble parts as well as in the secondary and service areas, deliberately designed, with a careful attention to itineraries; Even an overall underground network of carriageways and walkways were created so that traffic of vehicles and service personnel, which was certainly intense due the dimensions and functions of the villa, would not interfere with the main surface routes, for official and ceremonial use, eliminating at the same time noise, dust and traffic jams.

Indeed Villa Adriana was the site of an architectural experiment where consolidated aspects of roman tradition were re-elaborated into new and original combinations.

From the use and re-elaboration in ever so different ways of a few basic elements (porticoes, *exedrae*, rectangular, square and circular halls) derives the exceptional variety of architectural forms to be found in the Villa, characterized by the taste for monumentality, the search for scenographic so-

*Cryptoporticus*

## UNDERGROUND NETWORK

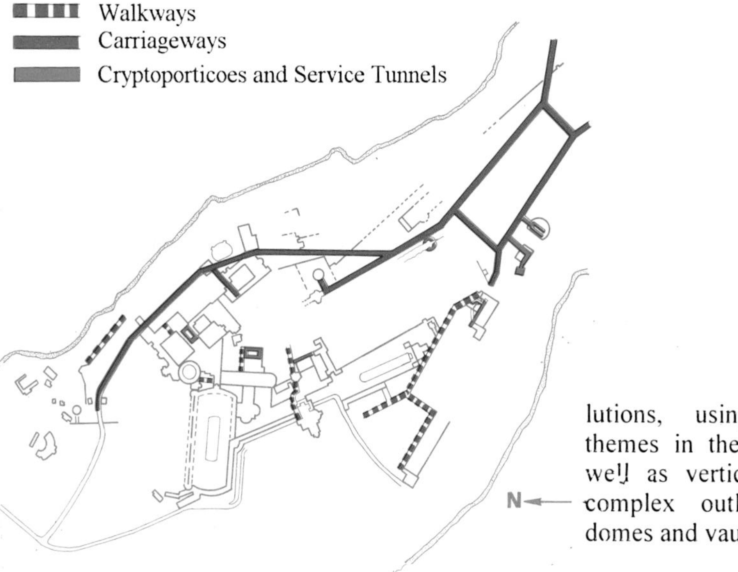


lutions, using curvilinear themes in the horizontal as well as vertical plans, and complex outlines for the domes and vaults.

## THE PECILE AND THE HUNDRED CHAMBERS

Originally the Pecile was constituted by only the double portico which closes the northern side of the present enormous space with the central pool. This grandiose portico extends itself on both sides of a central wall, which has been conserved up to a height of 9 m and having at each end circular passageways allowing to turn arounc the wall without coming out into the open. Being perfectly

*The Double Portico of the "Pecile"*

oriented East/West, the portico enabled one to exercise in all seasons, enjoying the cool shade of the northern side during summer and the warmer southern side during winter.

The vast court of grandiose proportions (230 x 96 m), was added subsequently, with the shorter sides slightly curved, surrounded by porticoes and occupied by gardens and a large central pool.

The entire western side of the complex rests on large sub-structures, more than 15 m high and constituted of a series of rooms (the so-called Hundred Chambers), built on various storeys (4 to the west and 3 to the south). The chambers, all having identical dimensions and not communicating in any way with the above porticoed enclosure were used as lodgings for slaves and the service personnel of the villa.

## THE APSED HALL KNOWN AS THE HALL OF THE PHILOSOPHERS

To the north-eastern end of the double portico of the Pecile, two short stairways lead into an imposing apsed hall, which is well preserved up to a considerable height. The main entrance was on the northern side, marked by two columns. In the apse, covered by a semidome, there are seven big rectangular niches, originally lined with marble, which according to a scholarly hypothesis, were to have contained the statues of the Seven Sages (from which comes the

*The "Pecile": reconstruction*

traditional name of the " Hall of the Philosophers "). In fact , the use of this hall is still uncertain and quite discussed. The presence of the niches suggested that it could have been used as a library. Their dimensions however, seem un-suitable to contain cupboards for the storage of papyrus books and parchments rolls, and are more appropriate for lodging a set of statues, which together with the precious marble decorations of the walls and floor, certainly gave the hall a rich and majestic aspect and could have assigned the hall to a highly ceremonial role (hall of the throne ?).

*The "Hall of the Philosophers"*

## THE ISLAND VILLA known as THE MARITIME THEATRE

This fanciful name was given in a completely arbitrary way to this singular building with a circular plan which was surrounded by a high outer wall which

*The "Maritime Theatre"*

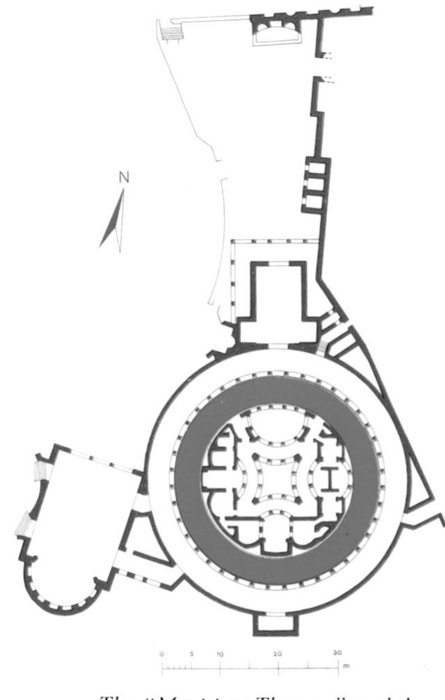


*The "Maritime Theatre" and the "Hall of the Philosophers": plan*



isolates it from the neighbouring buildings. Inside, one discovers a circular portico covered by a barrel vault supported by marble columns alongside a channel which delimits a small circular island on which is built a miniature villa. Two small wooden swing-bridges, which later gave place to the existing masonry bridge, allowed the access to the island.

Through a hemicycle vestibule, with lateral corridors, one entered into a small peristyle, with incurved sides and a central fountain, around which opened off numerous rooms: on the southern side a *tablinium* (or living room), with two adjoining symmetrical rooms (maybe rest rooms); on the western side a small bath building, comprising an *apodyterium* (dressing room), *frigidarium* (cold room) with a plunging tub and steps

*The "Maritime Theatre" reconstructio*

down into the canal, a *calidarium* (hot room) and a latrine; on the east a series of rooms maybe for a library.

The small and charming Island Villa, the model of which could be recognized in a building with a canal in the Palace of Dionysius the Elder in Syracuse, was probably used as a private summer residence of the Emperor. Fitted with all the amenities for comfortable living, the villa offered security and privacy which made it an ideal place for retirement and seclusion.

## THE CORTILE OF THE LIBRARIES, THE NYMPHAEUM, THE SUMMER TRICLINIA known as THE GREEK AND LATIN LIBRARIES

This complex takes its name from the two imposing buildings, which were mistaken for libraries, which dominate the northern side of a large peristyle with corinthian columns built by Hadrian over existing structures. Indeed the Nymphaeum on the northern side of the court belonged to the Republican villa, and was flanked by two corridors that link the peristyle with the artificial esplanade (the Upper Terrace) with gardens and many fountains, on which were raised the "Libraries".

Most probably they are two summer *triclinia* (dining halls) built over more than one level and linked by a trapezoidal portico.

*The "Greek Library"*

The "Greek Library", on the western side, comprised two intercommunicating halls, covered by cross-vaults, and characterised by the presence of large niches in the walls (three in the more inner hall, and four in the other). Various minor rooms are set around the building and from one of them a stairway leads to the upper storey.

The access to the "Latin Library" is through an ample vestibule with a curved façade, marked by columns. The first large hall, covered by a cross-vault, has niches on three sides.

Two twin corridors give access to the more internal room, covered with a barrel vault, on the back wall of which there is a large apse in which there is a statue base. A secondary atrium, flanked by a vestibule, was used to reach the rooms on the eastern side of the building which in origin also had a second storey.

*The Hospitalia*

## THE HOSPITALIA

The group of rooms known as the Hospitalia is eastwards from the Court of the Libraries: on the sides of a large corridor there are 10 rooms (five on each side) of the same dimension, each one having three alcoves, built to contain beds. Most probably this was a dormitory for the pretorians assigned to protect the main entrance of the Villa, built on this side.

All of these rooms contain charming black and white mosaics with geometrical and vegetal motifs. On the southern side are latrines and a large central hall, with a statue base, which can maybe be identified as a hall for the cult of the Emperor.

*The Hospitalia: mosaic with geometrical and floreal motifs*

# THE TERRACE OF TEMPE, THE LITTLE TEMPLE OF VENUS, THE GREEK THEATRE

*The Small Temple of Venus*

To the North-East of the so-called Hospitalia, was probably located the main entrance to the Villa. Here there are still imposing ruins, among which a great hall with a columned entrance-way, preceded by a portico flanked by three rooms on each side which could be identified as guard-posts.

The name of the famous valley in Thessaly was given to the vast artificial terrace which dominates the deep valley to the North-eastern side of the complex.

Going on towards North-West, one reaches the Little Temple of Venus, having a circular plan, and which is surrounded by a semi-circular portico which opens on to two large nymphaeums also semi-circular. The finding of a statue of Aphrodite of Cnidia (the one in-place is a moulded copy) has allowed to dedicate this small temple building to Venus, inspired by the Sanctuary of Cnidia, which housed the famous statue of the Goddess, sculpted by Praxiteles.

Slightly beyond, in an outside position, are the remains of the Greek Theatre, with an adjoining large rectangular court, with porticoes and maybe completed with a small temple on the cavea.

## THE IMPERIAL PALACE

On the southern side of the court of the " Libraries " there are the ruins of various structures (in *opus incertum*, *quasi reticulatum* and *reticulatum* works) belonging to the Republican age villa and subsequently englobed in the complex built by Hadrian called the Imperial Palace, part of which must have indeed been used for official ceremonies. Belonging to the most ancient period is the four-armed Criptoporticus which still conserves in its vaulted ceiling a great mosaic square made of marble chips , glass paste, shells, with figures of birds, vegetal, flower and geometrical motifs.

Towards the middle of the northern side, there is a portico leading to a large square *exedra*, transformed by Hadrian into a Library, which might have been the private one of the Emperor. On the eastern end there is a hall, divided into three naves by two lines of four columns and with a niche at the end wall, which due to its form and the rich decoration (which comprised, among other, the famous mosaic with the Centaur shown while hurling a rock against a tiger, now in Berlin), can be considered as a hall for the Emperor's audiences. On the eastern side there open a series of small rooms, preceded by a portico which served as bed-rooms.

The sequence of halls on the southern side are more complex and varied: eastwards a monumental entryway, semi-circular inside, leads to the so-called "Palace Nymphaeum" with porticoes on three sides and a stairway on the fourth.

In the centre were placed two oval-form fountains, which were added in a later phase when the building was transformed into nymphaeum. The particular layout and the monumental character of the structures led to suppose that originally it was used for meetings and spectacles.

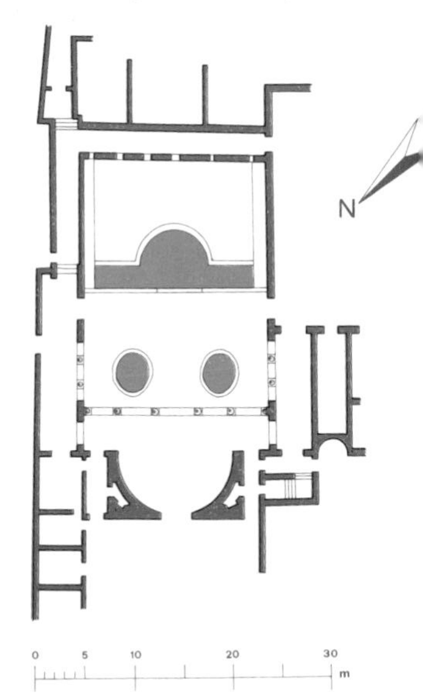


*Plan of the Palace-Nymphaeum*

Towards the opposite side there is the Summer Triclinium, a great dining hall, where an apse with niches can still be seen and at the base of which a channel and a *triclinium* bed runs in a semi-circle, similar to the so-called "Serapeo" of the Canopus.

*The Palace-Nymphaeum: exedra*

THE HALL OF THE DORIC PIERS

This building owes its name to the thin rectangular piers with fluted shafts and Doric capitals which decorate a large porticoed hall (32 x 23 m) built behind the "Imperial Palace". From here, through a rectangular room with columns between the door panels and the smaller rooms flanking it, one enters into another portico which surrounded an extensive open court, decorated with gardens and with a curving apse-like rear wall, with at its centre a statue-base. It is not quite clear what this complex was used for; certainly the rich marble decorations (floors in *opus sectile* and mosaics, and veneer walls) and the presence of a statue underline its function for ceremonies, accentuated by the axial lay-out of the rooms, which remind of the plans of the peristiles and the *triclinia* of Pompeian houses.

*Hall of the Doric Piers: detail of the entablature*

*Hall of the Doric Piers: reconstruction*

## THE BARRACKS OF THE VIGILES (FIREMEN)

The building which is located outside the "Imperial Palace", is composed of a great central hall, paved with bricks, on which open six rooms, with cross vaults, and of a hall which occupies the entire southern side, subdivided into three sectors each one also covered by a cross vault. A group of rooms including a latrine flanked the western side. Wooden balconies and steps connected the ground floor to an upper storey which rested on travertine corbels.

The modest quality of the structure is the best clue that its function was utilitarian. Called Barracks of the Vigiles due to its resemblance to a similar building in Ostia Antica, this complex was probably used for housing domestic personnel; a recent hypothesis states that it could have been a depot for food.

## THE "PIAZZA D'ORO"

The lavish ornaments and the wealth of works of art found in it have lead to give this building its name of "Piazza d'Oro" (the golden piazza), which undoubtedly is one of the most extraordinary of the whole Villa, due to the originality and the richness of the lay-out and architectural plans with very elaborate spatial solutions and exceptional structural levels.

*The "Piazza d'Oro": reconstruction of the northern side of the peristyle*

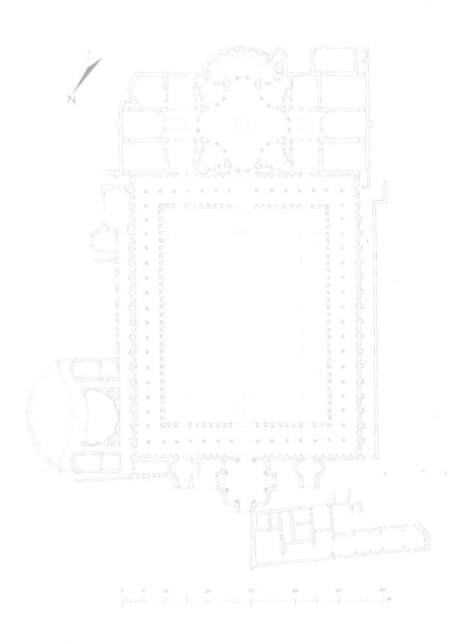


*The "Piazza d'Oro": general plan*



The main entrance, on the northern side, comprised a large octagonal vestibule; the walls opened alternately and with concave edged columns in-between onto semi-circular and rectangular niches the latter sur-

*The "Piazza d'Oro": "opus sectile" pavement*

mounted by large arched windows and with on the floor a square basin fountain.

This hall was covered by a beautiful umbrella vault springing from arches resting on entablatures held up by thin columns (now lost) set into plinths in masonry.

From the vestibule one enters into the large internal peristyle (61 x 51 m) laid out as a garden with a long central basin surrounded by a double portico held-up along the central aisle by columns and along the outer side by half-columns, enclosed by a wall decorated with small arches resting on columned walled pilasters. From the outside two long corridors, parallel to

*The "Piazza d'Oro": Vestibule*

the eastern and western sides, allowed to exit from the peristyle and linked it to the other parts of the complex without having to go through the main porticoes.

The most original structures are on the southern side: in the centre, in a dominating position, there is the great open-to-the-sky hall, with an alternatively concave and convex sided plan, marked by pavonazzetto columns. At each of the four corners there were domed apsed niches decorated with statues and water playing fountains which opened onto a great semi-circular nymphaeum with statues and fountains. There are covered rooms with rectangular or square plans symmetrically placed on each side of the hall preceded by a columned atrium with a central pool.

This very original complex of the Piazza d'Oro was probably an enormous and sumptuous pavilion for entertainment with gardens and fountains where banquets and receptions were held and was able to cater to hundreds of guests.

## THE HELIOCAMINUS BATHS

This complex built at the back of the "Imperial Palace" and of the court of the "Libraries", was the main thermal installation of the villa and gets its name from the round hall called Heliocaminus and mistakenly believed to be used for sun and sand bathing. The building is flanked on the north-eastern side by a long porticoed corridor opening onto three *apodyteria* (dressing rooms), towards the northern side there follows the *frigidarium*, a hall with an open air pool for cold baths, enclosed by a portico with

*The "Heliocaminus" Baths*

columns onto which opened a room with a front prospect of columns, with niches in the walls and a small semicircular pool for under-cover bathing. From here one entered into three rooms serving as *tepidarium* (warming-up) and after to the *calidarium* (for hot-water bathing). Towards the southern side is the so-called Heliocaminus: it consists of a vast circular hall, covered by a coffered dome and entirely occupied by a round basin with steps. Five large windows opened out on the south-western wall of the hall which was also equipped with a heating system using hot-air. These installations allow to identify the hall as a *sudatio*, that is a room for turkish baths.

## THE BUILDING WITH THE QUADRIPORTICO AND FISHPOOL AND THE NYMPHAEUM STADIUM

Even if located at different levels and built in different phases, these two buildings belong to a single enormous complex to which is also attached the building with the Three Exedrae, which has recently been identified as the Emperor's winter residence. The building with the quadriportico and fishpool is built on three levels. The upper one was the living quarters proper with large halls, richly decorated and heated. The fishpool, placed on this level was purely ornamental, decorated with statues and surrounded by a large portico held up by 40 columns. At the middle level were placed service rooms and passageways



*The Nymphaeum-Stadium: reconstruction of the northen sid*

and a four armed quadriportico, one of the better preserved of the whole villa, connected to corridors and stairways which gave access to the other floors: on its walls which had been coated with plaster and frescoed, can still be read the graffiti signatures of visitors and artists, some of them famous, of the XVIIth and XVIIIth centuries, among whom Piranesi. On the bottom floor in straight relationship with the Nymphaeum stadium were distributed several rooms, some of which richly decorated, maybe used for ceremonies or as monumental entryways. Recent excavations carried out in the building having the form of a *stadium*, have proven that in fact it was a great nymphaeum, subdivided into three sectors. The northern part, which one entered into through a long garden with porticoes on three sides and basins for water and plants is occupied by three rooms side by side. At the centre there is an open-air area with porticoes on two sides connected with the buildings flanking it. The southern part, with an open-air pavilion held up by columns and surrounded by a channel had at its end a great fountain with an *exedra*-like plan; the water fell from the steps of the half-circle and flowed through small channels to the front basin.

## BUILDING WITH THE THREE EXEDRAE

From the central area of the Nymphaeum stadium there was access into the building with the Three Exedrae which opens through a large hall onto the



*The Building with Three Exedrae: reconstruction*

southern portico of the Pecile entirely occupied by a fountain and flanked by two small porticoes. At the back there is an ample court, with porticoes on the eastern and western sides onto which opened three large porticoed semi-circled *exèdrae*. The eastern one opened onto to the east wing of the building which comprised a circular hall and two series of symmetrical rooms on each side.

The architectural decorations were rich and refined as attested by the remains of some column bases finely chiselled and capitals; the pavements were precious and elaborated with coloured marble intarsia (*opus sectile*) and the walls were faced with marble. It is common opinion that this luxurious complex must be identified with a great dining room (*cenatio*) for official banquets which was frequently compared to the majestic *Cenatio Iovis* of the *Domus Flavia* on the Palatine hill. However, a different hypothesis has been recently proposed concerning its function; according to it the building was to have been used as a monumental atrium entry-way to the Imperial residence which comprised as already mentioned, the Nymphaeum stadium and the Building with fishpool to which the small Baths were to be connected.

## THE SMALL BATHS

Going southwards, on the southern side of a vast open area, identified as a quadriportico connecting with the Nymphaeum Stadium, there is the view of the

*The Small Baths: detail of the painted vault*

oblique wall with three niches flanked by columns, enclosing the complex known as the Small Baths.

One enters them through a corridor, running parallel to an open-air court which was used as a palestra: from here one was led into the *frigidarium*, with two big apsed pools. A second corridor led to an octagonal hall (a changing room?), with sides alternately straight and convex, which held up a big segmented dome.

Towards west there is a round room (*sudatio* or

*calidarium*?), with niches and domed vault, communicating with various heated rooms, from which one entered into the great rectangular hall, entirely occupied by a pool with marble steps. Towards the south there is the *calidarium* with two rectangular pools, flanked by heated rooms which were used as *tepidarium*.

The precious and daring spatial and architectural solutions, the richness and preciousness of the pavements in *opus sectile* and of the wall facing have recently suggested that these baths were reserved for the Emperor and to a highly ranking public and therefore were part of the neighbouring residential complex.

In the past different opinions had been expressed, according to which the Small Baths were to have been the part reserved for women of a unique and enormous bathing complex used by the numerous personnel serving the Villa, which included the Large Baths, reserved instead to men, according to the ancient republican practice which forbid the use of the same baths by both sexes as attested by the bathing complexes of Pompei and Herculaneum.

## THE LARGE BATHS

This bathing complex was laid out a little to the south of the previous one from which it was separated by a complex and articulated building, the so-called vestibule, which was made up of porticoed areas and garden areas flanked by rooms, which were considered as a *gymnasium* and a *lararium* (seat of the

*The Large Baths: reconstruction of the frigidarium*

family Cult), or as a monumental entrance vestibule to the western part of the Villa (the Pecile and its neighbouring buildings).

One entered the Baths from the northern side, through a portico with columns which enclosed the open area of the Palestra, on which opened a great hall with rectangular niches; from here one entered the *frigidarium*, with two pools, rectangular on the north-eastern side, with niches for statues, and semi-circular on the western side, both preceded by cipollino columns. A curved corridor, at the far end of the western pool, leads to the heated rooms. At the centre of the south-western side is the imposing round hall, which probably had the function of a *sudatio*, at the south-east of which there were the *tepidarium*, the *calidarium* and the hall with the three basins. A series of underground corridors laid out under the western side gave access to the *praefurnia*, the ovens with boilers for heating the air.

The more modest quality of the wall and pavement decorations, the lesser care and preciousness of the architectural structures in respect of the smaller Baths, seem to be proof of the complex being for the use of the service personnel of the Villa.

*The Large Baths: frigidarium (detail)*

## THE PRAETORIUM

To the east of the Large Baths there is an imposing construction, the so-called Praetorium, placed as a containment wall of a vast artificial esplanade, in greater part unexplored, that southwards flanks the valley of the Canopus.

The building is composed of a series of rooms, obtained between the buttresses of the substruction walls, on three storeys and having access from an outside stairway placed at the western end. As they are similar to the Hundred Rooms, they must have been used as living quarters for the Villa's servants and maybe as depots and storehouses.

## THE CANOPUS

This is one of the most original and spectacular complexes of the villa, laid out in a long and suggestive small valley, flattened out and enclosed by a buttressed wall on the eastern side and with sub-structures on the opposite side, preceded by a series of rooms, originally used as living quarters for the service personnel and presently seat of the Museum of Villa Adriana.

At the centre of the valley there is a long water basin (111 x 18 m), with a curved side at its northern end, flanked by a corinthian colonnade which held up arched and rectangular alternated architraves. Parallel to the two long sides there are other two colonnades, double on the eastern side and single on the opposite site. At the centre of the western colonnade the columns are substituted by four caryatids (the original ones, found inside the basin, are shown in the Museum, and cement copies have been placed on site), copies of the Erechtheum of the Athens's Acropolis, and by two Silenae. Towards the northern side casts reproducing other statues have been placed: the Nile, the Tiber, a crocodile. In the spaces

*Caryatid from the "Canopus"*

*The "Canopus": reconstruction of the northern side*

between the columns there were copies of other statues from the age of Severus, Ares, Athena, Hermes and two Amazones (copies of those of the Artemision of Ephesus, which had been the works of Kresilas and Phidias).

South of the channel there is a big rectangular basin, flanked by two groups of rooms decorated by four columns with a curvilinear frame.

*Cocodrile from the "Canopus" (Villa Adriana Mus.)*

The far end of the valley is closed by a monumental nymphaeum with a semi-circular *exedra* (the so-called "Serapeo"), from the centre of which there is a long and imposing corridor leading to an apse. The great semi-circular hall, covered by a semidome, a "pumpkin" vault with alternately flattened and concave radiating segments, is animated by semicircular niches for statues and cascading fountains fed through a system of conduits by a small aqueduct on the outside. A couch with an inclined surface, obviously a *triclinium* bed (banqueting couch) ran around the

*exedra* wall and allows to identify the building as a summer *cenatio* (or banqueting hall).
On the sides of the *exedra* there are a series of rooms, of various forms and dimensions, maybe used for resting or as service quarters.

The identification of the complex with the Canopus as recorded by Hadrian's biographer seems exact: the plan, the architectural design and the decorations used are clearly inspired by the Egyptian world and evoke the original Canopus, the navigable channel leading off the Nile which linked Alexandria with the city of Canopus which was the seat of the celebrated Temple to Serapis, famous for the festivities and the banquets which were held there.

Therefore what is missing in Hadrian's creation is the building reserved for the

*The "Canopus": the large exedra or summer triclinium*

*Statue of Antinoos*

Cult itself; the great *cenatio*, used for sumptuous banquets and the plan of which is inspired by Egyptian Temples, is not, in any case, without elements related to the original model.

There is another recent interpretation, interesting and rich of suggestions, which sees in the Canopus a symbolic representation of the course of the Nile: the long corridor is the river itself, the small waterfalls are the cataracts, the *exedra* and the basin in front of it represent the Nile's Delta and the Mediterranean Sea bordered to the East, Ephesus (symbolized by the statues of the Amazons) and to the West by Athens (represented by the Caryatids).

Finally, no exclusion should be made to the hypothesis that the reference to the Nile and in general to the Eygptian world marks the precise will of the Emperor to make a tribute to his favourite, Antinous, who met his death right in the Nile, by building and dedicating him the Canopus.

## THE ACADEMY AND THE TOWER OF ROCCABRUNA

On the hill to the south of the Canopus, levelled by buttress walls, are the remains, unfortunately in a state of abandon, of the Academy. One entered this building through a great curvilinear atrium; this led into a vast peristyle with a double portico along a central wall, similar to that of the Pecile. Along the north-eastern side there are a succession of numerous halls which culminate with the so-called Temple of Apollo; a great circular hall, animated by brick semi-columns on which are set alternately rectangular and semi-circular niches.

Many works of art come from the Academy: among the most notable are the two black marble Centaurs, a Satyr in red marble, a Dyonysius (now in the Capitoline Museum in Rome). The preciousness of the statuary, the quality of the pavements (mosaic and *opus sectile*) and the features of the plan and architectural characteristics of the structures indicate that this building belonged to the noble part of the Villa and must have certainly been used for receptions and ceremonies.

Going on towards west, at the edge of a great artificially flattened out area contained by buttressed walls, the remains of a square plan building can be seen, with a monumental arched entrance which led into an octagonal hall. On the walls there are alternate rectangular and semicircular niches upon which rests a dome on the top of which there was in origin a circular pavilion with columns.

It was probably a belvedere tower from where a vast panorama could be viewed; It cannot be excluded that this tower, due to its structural characteristics, its isolated position and orientation could have been used as an observatory since Hadrian had a passion for astronomy.

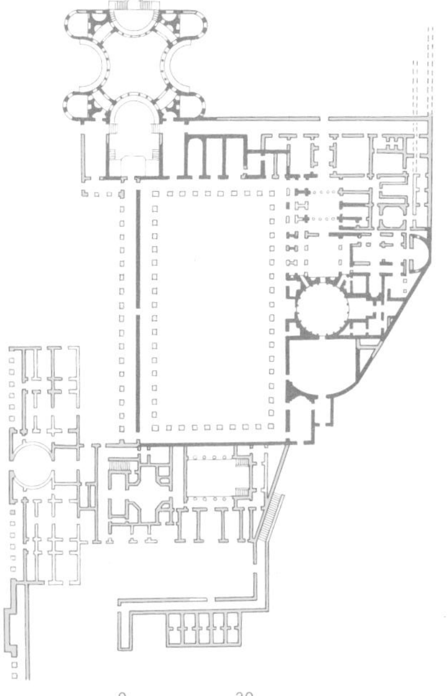


*The Academy: general plan*

# TIVOLI

## HISTORICAL SUMMARY

Located on the eastern margin of the Lazio plain, at the fixed point for passing from the higher to the lower valley of the Aniene river, ancient *Tibur*'s origins and history derive from its geographical location. The city, indeed, is said by legend to have been founded by the argivian heroes Catillus, Tibur and Cora, and was since the most far antiquity a halting place along the transhumance route from the coastal plain to the Apennine pastures and a strategic and commercial node along the natural transit route between Latium and the Abruzzi.

*Tibur* entered very early into contact with Rome, and after alternate episodes of clashes and alliances, it was definitively submitted in 338 B.C. at the end of the Latin war which brought Latium under the total rule of Rome. Having later become a municipality, the town, thanks to the beauty of its site and its relative closeness to Rome, became one of the most sought after vacation spots for the Rome aristocracy. Celebrated and famous characters of the political and cultural life of the capital, such as Julius Ceasar, Cassius, Brutus, Augustus, Maecenas, Horace, Catullus and many others built their villas in the pleasant surroundings of the city, the ruins of which still characterize to this date the landscape of Tivoli.

Before reaching the city, along the ancient route of the via Tiburtina, on the right hand side of the road are the remains of the so-called Temple of the Tosse, an imposing circular planned hall covered by a semidome. It probably was the monumental atrium entrance to a villa, that could be dated to around the IVth century A.D., and which was transformed during the Middle Ages into a place of church.

Going further along the Via Tiburtina one reaches the sanctuary of "Ercole Vincitore"

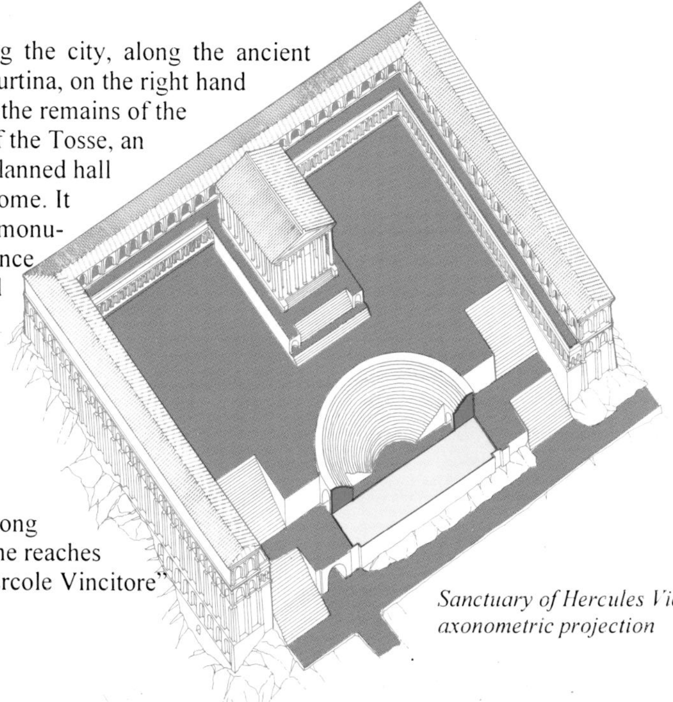

*Sanctuary of Hercules Victor: axonometric projection*

(the Victorious Hercules), which once was thought to be the villa of Maecenas. Already occupied during the XVth century by a convent, afterwards (in XVIII century) by an iron-works factory, then by a canon foundry and by other various factories, among which a paper factory which was recently dismantled, the complex is impressive due to its dimensions. These confirm the importance that was given by litterary sources to the sanctuary which had been erected towards the beginning of the 1st century B.C. and which was the seat of an oracle and of a cult among the most important of Latium, and which, originating right here in Tivoli, was later introduced into Rome during the late republican age. The better conserved part is constitued by grandiose constructions of *opus incertum* which sustain the enormous square where the place of cult was placed. A part of the via Tiburtina was incorporated within the construction, covered by a gallery (*via tecta*) and flanked by *tabernae* (i.e. shops). The big square (152 x 119 m) was surrounded on three sides by porticoes and on the fourth there was a theatre, opened onto the underlaying valley. At the back of the theatre's *cavea*, against the portico, there was a temple, raised on a high podium, with a three aisled cell.

The Via Tiburtina climbs up along a curvy route onto the western slopes of the Monte Ripoli on which is perched the city. The urban plan was strongly conditioned by the irregular morphology of the site; numerous terraces, sub-structions, stairs and ramps were built in many points to create building sites and to link the various levels. The Forum corresponded to the present-day Piazza del

Duomo and extended itself probably until the so-called Mercato, which in reality was an imposing subtruction that upheld the south-west side of the square.

## THE TEMPLES OF VESTA AND THE SYBIL

The acropolis of *Tibur* covers a spur that stretches out until the northern edge of the city, a rocky cliff almost sheer above the ancient falls of the Aniene river. Here are conserved the famous two small temples which have been attributed without any definite reason to Vesta and to the Sibyl, and which were turned into churches during the Middle ages. The most ancient which can be dated to the IInd century B.C. is the rectangular Temple, with a tetrastyle front of which two columns remain. The walls of the cella, in *opus quadratum* of travertine are decorated by ionic semicolumns. The round Temple, which is more recent (end of the IInd and beginning of the Ist centuries B.C.) was raised on an artificial platform in *opus incertum*, constituted by two superimposed orders of blind arches. The building, a peripteral structure with 18 Corinthian columns raises from a cement base faced with travertine slabs with hand-moulded frames. The entry portal with travertine door-jambs and lintel, is covered by a richly decorated frieze on which remains only part of the original dedicatory inscription. Inside the round cell, built in *opus incertum*, originally covered by rich stuccoes, one can note, in axis with the door, a small shrine, carved into the wall, faced

*The Temples of Vesta and of the Sybil: reconstructio*

with slabs of travertine with the pivot holes for the hinges of two small doors. On the outskirts of the city there was the Amphitheatre already known from an inscription found in the Sanctuary of Hercules, and the remains of which, datable to the age of Hadrian, have been located and partially uncovered northwards from the Rocca Pia. The ruins that can be seen are part of the northern side of the building, with the radial buttress walls which held up the overhanging tiers of seats, the circular ambulatory corridor and the two stairways that gave access to the upper floors of the *cavea*.

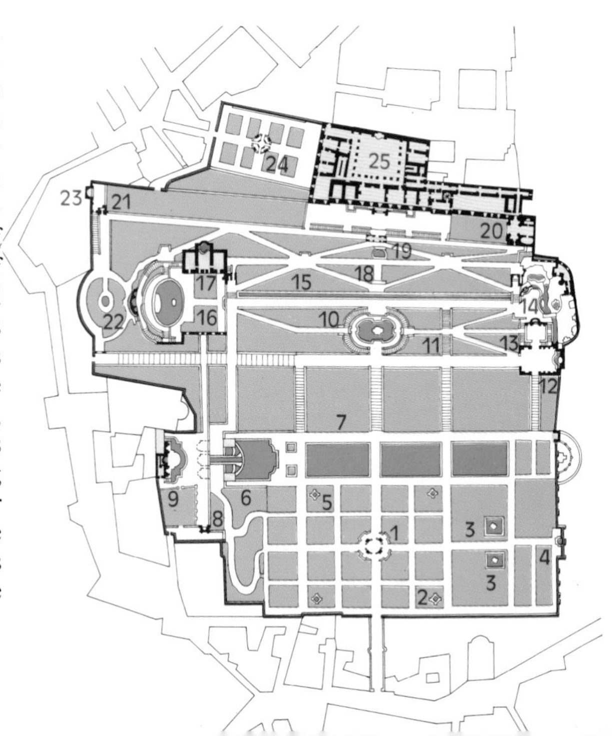

*The Villa d'Este: general plan*

*1 Cypress Rotunda*
*2 Fountain of Diana of Ephesus*
*3 Metae Sudantes*
*4 Fountain od the Swans*
*5 Fountain of the Eagles*
*6 Fountain of Neptune*
*7 Fishpools*
*8 Fountain of Venus*
*9 Fountain of the Organ*
*10 Fountain of the Dragons*
*11 Fountain of the "Bollori" (Boiling water)*
*12 Fountain of the Owl*
*13 Fountain of Proserpine*
*14 Fountain of Rome*
*15 Avenue of the Hundred "Fountains"*
*16 Fountain of the Ovato*
*17 Grotto of Venus*
*18 The Bicchierone Fountain*
*19 Fountain of Pandora*
*20 Grotto of Diana*
*21 Grotto of Aesculapius*
*22 Fountain of Pegasus*
*23 Fountain of Tethys*
*24 Secret Garden*
*25 Palace*

# THE VILLA D'ESTE

## HISTORICAL SUMMARY

The creator and founder of the villa was Cardinal Ippolito II d'Este (1508-1572), son of Alfonso I, third Duke of Ferrara and of Lucrezia Borgia.

A cultivated and intelligent man, brought up and educated in the sumptuous and refined atmosphere of the Court of the Estensi, one of the major political and cultural centres in Italy of its time, he was named Cardinal in 1538 and sent as the Pope's ambassador to France. Here he imposed himself on the court due to his political cleverness and to his friendship with the King François Ier.

Appointed by Pope Giulius III Governor of Tivoli, he entered the city in state in 1550 and took possession of the ancient Benedectine monastery neighbouring the church of S. Maria Maggiore (today S. Francesco), which seat of the city's government. Due to the tastes and refined habits of Ippolito II, who was used not only to the pomp and mundanity of the european courts, but who surrounded himself with powerful political figures, artists, scientists and writers, the residence that had been reserved for him must have appeared too modest and unsuitable for his rank. After not more than two months of his living in Tivoli he started the project that from thereon for twenty years would have led to the building of one of the most extraordinary and splendid Villas of the XVIth century.

In 1572 the Villa was completed; in the same year Ippolito II died. Having remained the property of the Este family, the enormous complex passed over through inheritances to the Hasburg family who did not take much care of the state and maintenance of the Villa. During the last century it was passed over to Cardinal Gustave von Hohenloe, who after carrying out the necessary restorations, gave hospitality to famous artists, politicians and persons of culture.

After the Peace Treaty of World War I, the villa became property of the Italian State which undertook important and complex repairs and opened it to the public.

## THE VILLA

The works on the villa began with the purchasing and expropriation of the lands flanking the convent which included the outskirts of the city suburbs and part of the underlaying valley (the valle Gaudente).

The plan which included the restructuration and enlarging of the monastery buildings and the creation of a vast garden along the steep slopes of the hill, was entrusted to Pirro Ligorio and built by the Ferrarese Architect G.A. Galvani.

The Palace, with a linear facade set-in between two projections on each side, is built on various levels, with a double loggia in the central part which links the two segments of the main stairway and gives access to the more important floors of the building, that with the private apartments of the Cardinal, and the one below for receptions.

Here is the great hall with the fountain, served on the back by a long criptoportico, certainly a reminder of Hadrian's Villa. The decorations attributed to Taddeo Zuccari, Girolamo Muziano and to their schools, were terminated by Federico Zuccari. On the right hand wall the original design of the villa is painted, flanked by two doors, a false one on the left, with the figure of a gentleman on the inside. At the centre of the vault there is a trompe-l'oeil perspective of columns holding-up the ceiling where a Banquet of the Gods is frescoed. On the left-hand wall, in a niche over the fountain there is a mosaic reproducing a typical view of Tivoli.

After there are four halls, with painted decorations depicting, in the first room mythological subjects, in the second allegories of nature, of the virtues, of the arts and sciences, together with busts of philosophers. The following hall is called the Glory of the Estes. The last room, called the hunting room, is frescoed by Tempesta, with hunting scenes set-into Tivoli's surrounding landscape.

The left wing of the floor for receptions is composed of five rooms; the first one completely frescoed with mythological scenes of the origins of *Tibur*, the work of Livio Agresti and his school; in the second one the chariot of Apollo and Venus is depicted on the vault, while the walls show scenes of the sources and rivers of Tivoli and the stories of King Anio. The next room shows Noah's sacrifice; the fourth tells of the stories of Moses. The last one is called the room of the crèche due to the presence of a Nativity scene in a niche.

After climbing two flights of stairs, one enters the so-called old apartment, composed of ten rooms, which in the original project were to have been decorated with sixteen tapestries with the story of the Mythological Hippolytus, which had been commissioned to Pirro Ligorio, who however only made sketches and descriptions. All of the rooms are frescoed by Agresti and his school. Noteworthy is also the neighbouring chapel, rich in stucco works and friezes.

## THE GARDEN

It undoubtedly represents, the most complete model of a renaissance garden, a perfect combination of architecture and nature. The XVIth century garden, in-

*The Fountain of the Hydraulic Organ*

deed, is before anything else, a work of architecture, conceived along precise geometrical rules and principles, in order to mould and model nature, tracing perfectly straight avenues, squared off terraces and flower-beds, thus creating rigid symmetry and carefully studied perspectives; at the same time it is the ideal site for fanciful formal solutions and scenographic effects, combining the tree elements with sculpture, painting, music, sound and especially with the flow of water.

The garden of Villa d'Este occupies the vast and steep slope which descends from the Palazzo, by means of ramps and avenues, to a bottom terrace, where the entrance for those coming from the

Via Tiburtina was. Not few technical problems had to be solved to create enough space for the elaborate architectural designs as well as to assure enough water supply for feeding the fountains, water falls and water jets. The system for catching and distributing the water from the Aniene river, is a real masterpiece of hydraulic engineering, thanks to which even today , the fifty fountains present in the garden can still offer spectacular water-playing effects.

From the double ramp of the great master stairway of the Palace, one descends leftwards to reach a circular piazza: here is the fountain of Pegasus. The mythical winged horse is represented in the position of taking a leap to fly away from a big rock on which he rests his back hoofs with his wings spread.

Leaving this square one reaches the Fountain of the Organ: four *telamones* with folded arms mark the front perspective with niches and statues of Apollo and Orpheus, and hold-up the decorated entablature crowned by an eagle , the heraldic device of the d'Este family. During the XVIIth century a small pavilion was inserted into the central niche, in the place of the statue of Diane of Ephesus (now standing at the end of the garden), to protect the hydraulic organ. The violent falling of the water into a cavity made the air come out of the organ pipes at the same time another water device moved the keys to produce harmonious sounds.

One proceeds onto the Cypress Rotunda, originally occupied by a pavilion surrounded by flower form fountains. At the edge of the park is the Fountain of

*The Fountain of Hydraulic Organ: Façade*

Nature with a statue of Diana of Ephesus coming from the Fountain of the Organ: from the numerous breasts of the goddess, which symbolize fecundity, gush spurts of water.

A little beyond is the Fountain of the Mete made up of great and shapeless blocks of rocks stacked on top of each other which ooze water, in imitation of the Meta Sudante, the gigantic roman fountain placed along side the Arch of Constantine, in Rome, in the valley of the Coliseum.

Going beyond the mutilated Fountain of Ariadne, the zone of the fishpools is reached; they were three great basins which were used to raise trout and other fresh water table fish.

Walking along the left side of the fishpools, one can see, in a parallel avenue, the Fountain of Eagles, with four of the birds of prey, heraldic symbols of the House of d'Este inserted in the family's coat-of-arms.

*The Fishpools*

The Fountain of Neptune, which closes the sequence of the fishpools, was built in 1927 and in it was placed the statue of the Sea god which had been part of a gigantic group of statues conceived for a fountain which had been foreseen in the original project but which was never completed.

In climbing to the upper terrace, there is in axis with the central avenue crossing the whole garden, the Fountain of the Dragons, a work of Pirro Ligorio. At the centre of the great basin, enclosed by two imposing amphitheatre-like flights of steps, is the

*The Fountain of the Dragons: Façade*

monument that gives its name to the complex: four winged dragons, from whose jaws spurt strong jets of water. the group was placed here to honour the visit of Pope Gregory XIII Boncompagni, whose heraldic device was precisely a dragon. The fountain designer Tommaso da Siena contrived that the water, on emergence made the sounds alternately of canon shot and arquebus fire.

At the end of the avenue of the hortensias is the Fountain of the Owl, the work of Giovanni del Luca and of Raffaello Sangallo. In the centre there is a big niche flanked by two columns covered with mosaics with vine garlands and golden apples; on the attic storey there are two female figures alongside a central panel with angels which hold up the coat-of-arms of Ippolito IInd. Unfortunately nowadays the ingenious device that was

*The Fountain of the Owl*

*The Fountain of Proserpine: Façade*

in the niche and moved by water emitted the screeching of an owl and bird songs, has disappeared.

A little to the left, towards the Palace, there is the Fountain of Proserpine, which was the back-drop of a open air dining room; In it was placed, in the XVIIth century, a stucco group representing Proserpine abducted by Pluto and transported to the infernal cavern on a boat in the form of a shell.

The long stairway which leads to the avenue of the Hundred Fountains, called the Cordon of Boiling water, presents on the parapet plinth forty-two low spurts which give the effect of boiling water.

From the Fountain of Proserpine the so-called Rometta is reached, a highly original complex which consists of miniature reproductions of the most important buildings of ancient Rome (the Pantheon, Augustus's Mausoleum, the Coliseum etc.). The personification of the Aniene and Tiber rivers can be recognized. Along the latter can be noted a small island in the shape of a ship representing the Tiber Island. At the centre there is the statue of goddess Roma accompanied by the she-wolf feeding the twins Romulus and Remus. The fountain, devised like the others by Pirro Ligorio, served as a permanent backdrop of a small open-air theatre which fell into ruins and was demolished during the last century.

*"The Rometta"*

The avenue of the Hundred Fountains is famous, with twenty-two small boat-like fountains, alternated with obelisks and lilies (which together with eagles are part of the coat-of-arms of the

*"The Rometta":*
*detail of the upper miniature-monuments*

*Statue of Rome*

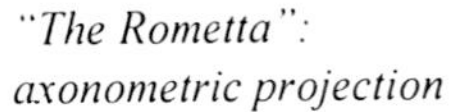

*"The Rometta": axonometric projection*

*1 Entrance*
*2 Fountain of Proserpine*
*3 Square*
*4 Eastern Side*
*5 Tiber Island*
*6 Bridge*
*7 She-wolf*
*8 Statue of Rome*
*9 Elliptic balcony*
*10 Tiber*
*11 Circular Monument*
*12 Porta Flaminia*
*13 Statue of Tiber*
*14 Apennines*
*15 Anio Vetus*
*16 Upper miniature-Monuments*

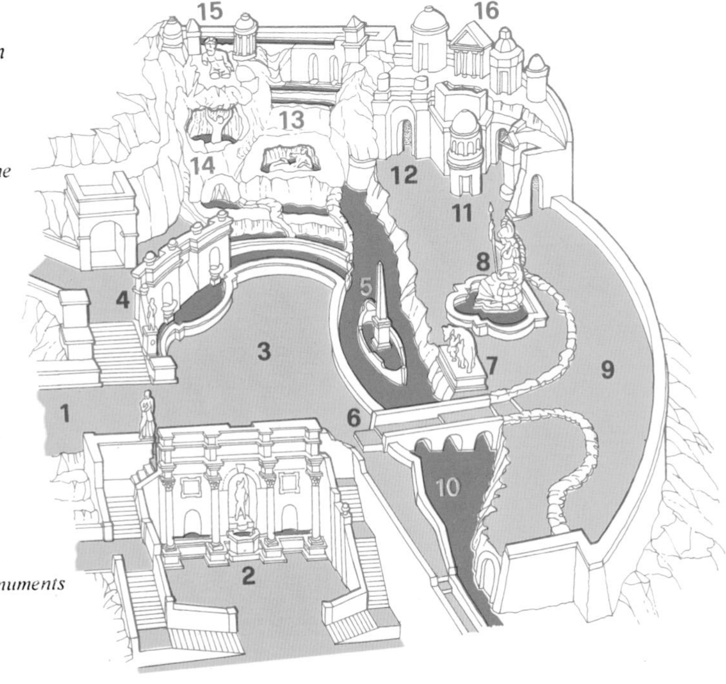

*The "Hundred Fountains"*

d'Este family) fed from three channels with hundreds of small spurts and in origin decorated with coloured stuccoes showing mythological scenes from the Metamorphoses of Ovid.

Going down the whole length of the avenue one reaches the Fountain of the Ovato which is certainly the finest of the villa. Here architecture, nature and fantasy blend together in an admirable harmony.

The great fan of water plunging into the basin below alludes to the Aniene river falls, the grottoes the mountain above Tivoli and the statues placed in it to the three rivers within. the Tivoli territory. Underneath is a large semicircular basin, adorned with ten statues of nymphs placed in the niches that alternate to the arches of a portico standing behind which can be walked through and suggestive of walking under water.

Not far away is the Fountain of Bacchus that has today lost the statues that once adorned it.

Still walking up the garden one reaches the Bicchierone Fountain, made of a huge shell upholding a flower trophy in travertine down which the water flows.

Finally one reaches the Grotto of Diana, with rich decorations in coloured stucco, mosaics and bas-reliefs with mythological scenes.

This extraordinary site is highly suggestive, as it was conceived for the enjoyment of nature and of beauty; it is an admirable work and symbol of XVIth century architecture, where the regularity and rigidity of the garden's plan, with orthogonal axes is diluted by the variety of

*The "Rometta" Fountain: statue of the Aniene river*

the vegetation , the architectural and plastic forms of the fountains and in the fantastic and scenic use of water, considered like nature, as an element to be modelled as one pleased.

In making their choices during the design of the villa, all of those who worked there were under the considerable influence of ancient architecture, and in particular of the suggestive ruins of Hadrian's Villa, where right during those years great excavations and the recovery of exceptional works of art were being carried out. Pirro Ligorio actively participated in these works, and he drew and described the greater part of the buildings and of the statues as they were being discovered. Many of the latter ended up in the Villa of Ippolito IInd and were subsequently dispersed.

*The Fountain of the Ovato*

The very original architecture of Hadrian's Villa must have inspired not single parts of the Cardinal's residence but instead the whole general architectural concept which, like the Imperial Villa is the result of a perfect balance between green spaces and buildings.

*The Fountain of the Ovato: detail of the central fall*

# BUILDING TECHNIQUES USED IN VILLA ADRIANA

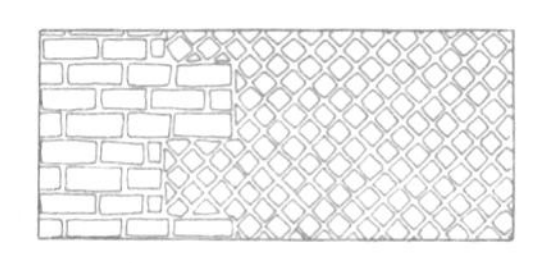

1. *Opus reticulatum.* Walling of concrete faced with squared-off stones arranged on diagonal lines like fish net meshes. Already used in Rome and Central-southern Italy since the end of the 2nd - beginning 1st centuries B.C., this technique continued to be applied until the early Imperial age.

2. *Opus testaceum* (or *latericium*). The use of bricks baked in an oven (*testae*) is applied since the first Imperial age. Made in a square form they were then cut into triangles before their laying in place.

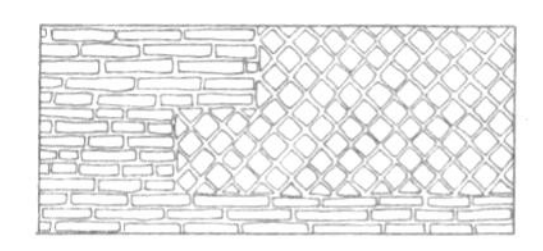

3. *Opus mixtum.* Walling in concrete constitued of alternated bricks and *opus reticulatum* courses. This technique used from the 1st century A.D., is the most widely applied in Villa Adriana.

4. *Opus vittatum.* Walling made of courses of small rectangular stone blocks (usually tufa) alternated with courses of bricks. Used already during the first half of the II century A.D. at Villa Adriana (in the Roccabruna building), this technique widely spread during the Late Antique age.

ROMA Come era e come è
CON RICOSTRUZIONE DEI MONUMENTI ANTICHI

VILLA ADRIANA
TIVOLI E VILLA D'ESTE

OSTIA ANTICA

CATACOMBE DI ROMA
E NECROPOLI VATICANA

POMPEI·ERCOLANO
E VILLA IOVIS A CAPRI

PAESTUM

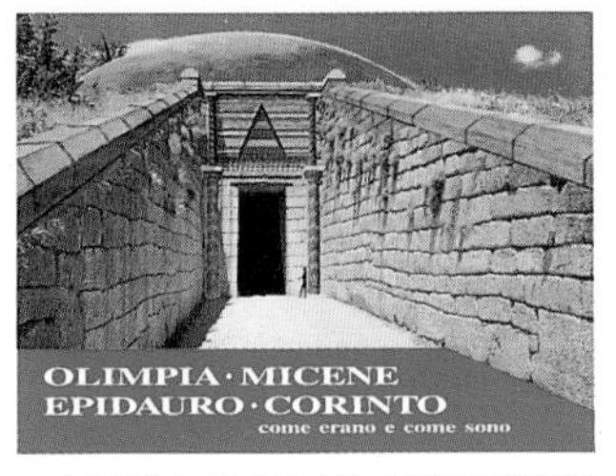

# SERIES "GUIDES WITH RECONSTRUCTION"

In English, German, French, Italian, Japanese, Spanish, Greek. With the **Vision** system each volume includes a series of plates reconstructing the ancient artifact printed on a transparent overlay wich integrates and completes the missing parts of the underlaying photograph of the monuments as seen today. To better understand the ancient world.

VISION s.r.l. – Via Livorno 20 – 00162 Rome (Italy)- Tel/Fax (39) 0644292688
E-mail: info@visionpubl.com

PAST & PRESENT®



ISBN: 88-8162-014-6

*Printed in Italy by La Zincografica Fiorentina – Interplastic Print*